Haunting the Winerunner

Man was not created for the sake of discovering the absolute truth. The absolute truth has its own intangible reality and scorns to be known. The function of mind is rather to increase the wealth of the universe, in this special dimension, by adding appearance to substance and passion to necessity and by creating all those private perspectives, and those emotions of wonder, adventure, curiosity, and laughter which omniscience would exclude.

— *George Santayana*

For Ben, Jack, and Susan.

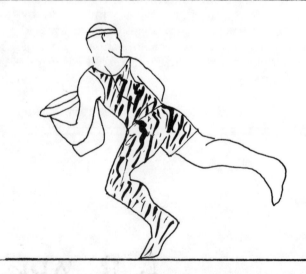

Haunting
the Winerunner

Poems by John Wink
With illustrations by Linda Brown

Parkhurst/Little Rock
PUBLISHERS

Library of Congress Catalog Card Number: 82-083161
    Wink, John
    Haunting the Winerunner
    Parkhurst: Little Rock
    October, 1982

ISBN 0-941780-14-7

This is an original paperback edition.

Of the poems included in this volume, the following have
appeared in the following places:

"Wayne's Cream Wheat Poem" *Stone Drum*
"Love" *Moondance*
"Saved But" *Voices International*
"Poem From A Godly Angle" *Voices International*
"What If" *The Windless Orchard*
"Pool" *The Windless Orchard*
"Slightly Contra Freud" *Cycloflame*
"Why Jack Butler Is An Occasional Junk Reader" *Corduroy*
"An American English Teacher Foresees His Craft"
      Grapevine
"Written At His Grandmother's Grave" *Voices International*
"Dining At The Vishnu" *Grapevine*
"Movies Are Pleasant. They Have Endings." *Grapevine*
"When Jesus Walked The Waters" *Grapevine*
"Stinkfed Clams" *Grapevine*
"After Having Read Malcolm Cowley's Account . . ." *Kansas
      Quarterly*
"Small Kafkaesque" *Lucille*

The poet gratefully acknowledges the permission of the
editors of the above journals to reprint these poems.

TABLE OF CONTENTS

PART FOUR: AMATEUR METAPHYSICS

PART FIVE: AUTOBIOGRAPHY

Preface by Jack Butler

I've been thinking about John Wink's poetry for years. He is my friend, and I may as well say up front that the worst thing I can think of to say about him is that he is a secular humanist.

And we know what they're like.

I've been thinking about John Wink's poetry for years because I have loved his poetry for years. I always saw myself in this role, someday, too: Someday I would be writing a preface for a book of his poetry, I would be preparing the way for him, I would be explaining him to the world. As far as off the wall goes, I always thought he invented the wall. The first time I ever saw him, he was bouncing things off walls and catching them, playing wonderful and totally unexpected little games.

Such are the presumptions of friendship. Only recently has it begun to come clear to me that this fellow needs no precursors, no earnest explainers. I think maybe the world is ready. I think there just may be a whole crowd of people who can go right with him, right down to Burnt Sienna, right down to brunch at the Vishnu, where the menu is divine, and the recipes are like nothing else anywhere.

That I think I can say: Nobody else writes at all like this, nobody else comes at things in such — such a *Winkian* mode.

Now I can relax, now that I've gotten the word "mode" into this preface. "Mode" is a serious intellectual word. Using it ought to prove that this is serious intellectual poetry.

We've established him as intellectually serious, and he doesn't need explaining. That leaves a prefacer with almost nothing to do but tell you a few of the things he likes about the poetry. Johnny Wink loves to make lists. It should serve him right to be prefaced by a list, then.

Twenty of my three favorite things in John Wink's poetry:

7

1. The first poem in the book, all of it. A beautifully done sonnet. "The World" indeed. I love the line "A thin man hawks a complex paradise," its stresses, how "hawks" and "complex" sound off each other. I love how directly it gets at the trouble we have trying to explain the world to each other: "O what is bad, dispensers, what is good?" "Out here it's dog-eat-dog. All men are brothers." Beautiful, beautiful.

2. The way phrases grab hold of him and spirit him off. "Fish out of water," for example: We all use it, but he creates it, he puts them in pines and in "the foul chokecherry." And as often as not, the idiosyncratic little maps he makes to follow such phrases to their oddest reaches will lead him into something more than strange, more than fetchingly different, will lead him into having said, as he does in this poem, something strong about our lives.

3. He gets his revenge on English by grabbing hold of it in turn. I love him because he can misunderstand his way into haunting the winerunner, because, winerunner that he is, he can wake up haunted by the logic of a dream in a poem like "Nightwood," and get it down, get just a whiff of that utterly real realm but so forgettable, get it into my nostrils before it goes. I can't say I love the way he will sometimes insist that what we have done in the twentieth century is mugged a gila monster. He *will* insist sometimes. On that matter, I stand with Dr. Susan Wink, the lady with the butcher knife. But on balance, if we have to have "mugged a gila monster" in order to get Attila the Hunchback, or creamworks, or stink-fed clams — well, then, I approve.

4. His shrewd eye, his refusal to be budged. When he talks about when Jesus walked the waters, he doesn't worry about the big deal, doesn't hate miracles or go sappy with love for them either. He wants to ask disturbing little questions someone should have thought of a long time ago: "How?" That's the entire first line of "When Jesus Walked the Waters." "Did you select/ A surfer's style and slide and glide/ ... ?" he asks. "Or did you perpetrate a ghostly surface/ Two feet or so below the cruel crests/ And slosh along, a weird pedestrian?" Try getting those images, that question, out of your mind.

5. How long the gentle, hookfaced pool-player's run has lasted.

6. "They creamed a man in Chapultapec, Señor."
7. His reverence. Here is a man who loves God, who loves all the God he can get. Of course, if you don't think it is proper to love God and be a humanist, if you think it is just terrible to have a strong mind capable of doubt and irony as well as appreciation, you shouldn't be reading these poems. But if you think that just maybe what the almighty creator of the universe wants is something a little more than a crowd of cheery zombies rendering him continual applause, his very own laugh-track, you might want to spend a long time in the section of this book called "Amateur Metaphysics." "Dialogues with God" sees Him as anything but Kathy's clown. "Bad Animals on the Baltic" has something to say about intolerance. Find the Old Testament and the New on one page in "Jesus Loves You. But Does God Love You?" Think about the title of "Saved, But" — then read it.
8. "Poem from a Godly Angle." I know I'm cheating — this is really part of number 7. But it is worth an individual mention.
9. His way with words. Partly it is traditional skill — the ability to get all sadness in "The kind sun was wasting my life," or the *in's* he gets in the penultimate line of "The Kingdom of God . . . ," the resonance of meaning in the word "mortified" in "Poem from a Godly Angle," or how perfectly suited the long word for a short thing, "infinites-imality," is in that same poem. Partly it is the weird phrases he allows to exist in his mind, which I have already mentioned. But there is a sort of always unexpected and often almost unnoticeable little difference that is a result of how he sees things. I am thinking of lines like "Best love boils to imagination" in the last poem of the book. Almost anybody else in the world would have said, "Boils *down* to imagination." But he sides with the distillate, not the sludge.
10. His sense of the strangeness of things, the tiny ruptures "barely moving in normalcy's womb." And his way of handling them, the beer cans he flattens out to read at breakfast. "Small Kafkaesque" does justice to this sometimes chillingly disjointed construct we call reality.
11. Sex.
12. Friends and family. Domesticity is here, and made valuable to read about. People are here, in their own persons

and in some rather bizarre persons the poet has thought up for them whether they like it or not. So much of a good life must be domestic. To live with others well is to learn to adventure in the small things, to celebrate them truly.

13. The delicious mockery he makes of willful ignorance, his humility in the face of his own ignorance, his gentleness with simple human confusion. Everyone who has ever taught or taken a liberal arts course should read "The Renaissance Humanities Course Multiple Choice ... ," one of the funniest poems I've ever read. And dearest. "Jane Austen" may gain a little if you know that its author has tried (often successfully) to teach that witty novelist to many a class of blacks and whites and Christians. Regardless, it has something wonderful to say about soul, and who has it, and it has a wonderful time saying it.

14. Imagination. For John Wink, imagination is more than a nice little attribute you want your children to have if they have the time. It redefines and creates the world and love. "The World" and its contradictory doctrines begin this book: It ends with "Love," a kind of answer, and "Best love boils to imagination." Imagination freshens. Our little games are our hearts.

15. His appreciation: of Jane Austen, the Ouachita Tigers' basketball team, true learning, roast beef and furious thighs.

16. "On a clear day you can get your ass whipped/ The daddy honkers said ... "

17. Two mystics pruning a grapefruit.

Seventeen is enough. I like seventeen. I'll just list seventeen of the twenty of my three favorite things about John Wink's poetry. The only word I haven't used in here that I'm sorry I haven't used in here is "idiolect." He has a hell of an idiolect, and I wish I had worked that word in somehow.

I hope you're the kind who reads prefaces last. If you are, you're probably coming to this wishing you could write one of your own for the book. Do. Let's all write a preface for *Haunting the Winerunner* and mail it to him. I suggest a cover letter to go with it, beginning, "Dear John Wink: I have read your poems and liked them very much and wrote this preface for you. Please send me ten dollars."

Jack Butler

PART ONE:
THE WORLD

The World

The World

They'll sell you anything in these mean streets.
A thin man hawks a complex paradise,
A hill of purges and a hell of ice.
A self-taught man named Epicurus treats
Of happiness and deems serenity
The highest pleasure. He gets misunderstood.
O what is bad, dispensers, what is good?
A German pushes relativity.
You will not know exactly what you've bought
From Jews, Italians, Greeks and others
In this obscure and sorely vexed domain.
Out here it's dog-eat-dog. All men are brothers.
Uncertainty's the principal refrain.
All longing's from the stars. Or from the gut.

Fish Out Of Water

The jackfish swimming through the piney woods
Grow lopsided in the absence of their air.
Tonight the seas are dark and bare.

The bantam shrimp! I glory in their style,
A sleek propulsion through the foul chokecherry.
Their wriggling makes this old heart merry.

I louder sing the trap the mako's in.
He's in a tattered trap for sure, the blue marauder.
The brambles now engulf him. Lovely slaughter.

The bonefish goes about the gum. The gum is dark.
The bonefish goes so very far
From where his fellows are.

Or were. Tonight the seas are dark and bare.
The speckled trout succumbs. The winsome peach
Has got him in her clutches, plans to teach

Him much of what it is to land on land,
Of what a way we have with tangled misery
And rot and drought and all that isn't sea.

Stink-fed Clams

Nothing was ever quite so awful as stink-fed clams.
I know the orthodontists plugged them,
And the health nuts, too.
Still, I could never tell my freshmen
They were the thing to do.

Yet they came to me with all this talk, this rumbling,
Stink-fed clams this, stink-fed clams that.
They say in the East that stink-fed clams are going down,
Coming on, putting out, making tracks.
Then they cut me brutally, saying,
"Where's your sense of style, boy?"

Fled long ago, I guess.
Gone with Attila the Hunchback and Ron Rico
To a hunting ground happy sans stink-fed clams.

He Laments Carlsbad Caverns
And The Things
That Cannot Happen There

They have conquered Carlsbad Caverns, chipped it down
To something full of paths and johns and cokes.
No one screams but babies. Nothing croaks
Or snarls or lumbers crookedly. No one frowns.
This one's staggered, that one's quite amazed.
"Fascinating" vies with "fabulous."
But, though the viewers make a chortled fuss,
A flashbulb shows their eager eyes are glazed.

I fail to find a tourist who espies
Monsters, explorers' bones or just Pat Boone.
I'll take my chances with the waning moon,
Whose junk is still well-hidden from my eyes,
Whose memory is still in poets' blood,
Which drips and dries in Carlsbads' prosy mud.

Poem Inspired By Simultaneously Reading
The Alpha Chi Constitution And
Listening To Inexpressibly Corny People
Rattle On On The Johnny Carson Show

On a clear day you can get your ass whipped,
The daddy honkers said,
Then flew away.
Sometimes they're so bad they make you feel good,
But then they leave and a commercial comes on.
(And I don't care what they say; I cannot build a viable
    myth
Out of Pfeifer Plumbing and Gas.)
An actress who looks profound says,
"Did you see me in 'The Thing With Two Heads'?"

Then they all leave forever
And you are left with "The National Anthem"
And God.

Loss

Though all the trees on the riverbank
Have accepted spring again
With practiced nods of green,

The view from here spells loss —
It slices the air.
All is loss out there!

Loss freights and fugues the atmosphere,
Roars its balances,
Shouts its counterpoints.

Pool

Fast Eddie good Bruce better man I knew this fatguy
Once took Wichita Slim and he was fine, so fine

Somewhere in faraway Tacoma
A gentle, hookfaced man is shooting pool.
He carries about him the last vital essence of cool:
He is six foot four, eats the best pretzels,
Drinks Olympia lager beer.
For ten long years
He hasn't missed.

For The Ouachita Tigers' Basketball Team: A Request

The paraplegic in his mobile chair
Is never going to walk away from it
Without your help. The fellow there
Up high — see him — in the stands,
The pasty-faced guy with the hopeless glands:

How will he ever be svelte
Without your glistening help?

That old, old lady on the front row
Won't last long in any case.
Bring her to her feet once more
Before the darkness lays her down.

Remind her that life
Is a leaping affair,
A time that may shine

And let her make your shining leaping hers.

Movies Are Pleasant. They Have Endings.

When the handsome, pained man in the silk white shirt
Enters the Pancake House to the tune of a stirring song,
You know he'll either die in a pool of gun-sponsored blood
Or round off his life in a word, a phrase, a minor myth.

The cameras scream, "No more life for you!
Your life is finished, wrapped in mummycloth."

PART TWO:
FRIENDS AND FAMILY

Easter Susan

You went so well with the background —
The heath, profound in its brief distance,
The green that sung in the trees,
The colored wash of eggs
That sponsored this day's joy.

I saw you still carried a wound about,
A complex wound that many weapons made.
(And yet your belly is still ripe for love,
Your eyes are still bright as they are dark,
The hint of adventure still roars about your many passages,
Still whirls about your carriage.)

When you went in with our son
To eat uncovered hard-boiled eggs,
The landscape's body reported your going.
Something had been plucked from the finished anatomy.

A vulgar cowbird replaced you.
The sky bled a gray cloud
And it stained the sun.

This Chiropractor Came Wandering

through a story I was only half listening to,
into the motions of my troubled mind
he came wandering,
into my love life,
into my lovely wife
he came, probing her golden sorrows

Partings

This moment is full of fear.
We are trying to make it habitable.
Susan has filled it with a new dress
And a silver pin in bunned hair
Above her swanny neck —
She is dazzling.
Talk of ginger lilies and African violets
Fills this frightened air.
Coffee makes the moment nearly comfortable.
The clock says nothing but fear.

On Refalling In Love With His Wife

The saddest thing in all of this
Is how in others' eyes I miss
Your eyes. Unfair of life
To take from life. And you, my wife,
Have eaten all my helpless heart
In innocence. My other life will start
Again. I'll hear a click, a rattle.
What isn't you won't seem such tiresome prattle.

Mugged A Gila Monster

I develop theories at night
On the toilet, on my way
To get my son a cheese sandwich.
For weeks "mugged a gila monster"
Has run in my head.
I take it seriously
Because nothing is given in vain.
Last night, on the way
To turn the furnace to sixty-two degrees,
I received the meaning of the image
And relayed it to my wife
As soon as I attained the bed:
"Somehow it's what we've *done* in the twentieth century."
"Somehow I don't see it quite that way."

Sometimes

I make it rough on my wife sometimes.
The other night, for instance, I insisted
"I desired my dust to be mingled with yours
Forever and forever and forever" is the best
Thing ever in poetry.

She agreed.

I said, "Anybody who doesn't agree is both cruel
And a communist," and tried to force another concession.

I said, "I make it rough on you sometimes, don't I?"

She was cooking rice and beans.
She had a butcher knife in her hand.
She smiled.
She said, "Sometimes."

Recurring Dream

I walked into the world of women.
I trembled.
They were all taller than I.

And once, picking Gene up at school,
I saw him, seven years old
(I saw him in the rear view mirror),
And behind him (in the rear view
Mirror) came the junior high school women
In blue jeans with lean and hungry walks.

I was afraid for him.

Gene's Tale

He said he rode to Mexico to be with the cows.
He rode over some high rivers and met a dinosaur
But didn't kill him; instead he cured him
With medicine, of a hurt heart,
For which kindness the dinosaur gave him
A dinosaur-back ride, he claimed.

In The Town Of Burnt Sienna

Sometimes the blessings heap almost too high.
In love with my wife, in the kitchen with my wife,
I had a hunger dream of roast beef and furious thighs.
Then son Gene spun in his verbal green
And, spotting two biscuits, said, "Two mystics."
I turned to the open door
(We were letting everything in that night
And everything seemed to be getting in).

There weren't two mystics,
But there were almost two mystics.
There was almost everything I'd ever need
That night, in the town of Burnt Sienna.

Jack Butler: Split End In Outer Space

Suppose you came back to planet Earth, dear Jack,
And we were huddling in Antarctica
And I blew on my hands and called flexrightX26ontwo.

Say you
Were split right and Bob was split left.

On two you left,
Gone in the good confidence that the snap,
My deep drop and the blocking would all be there.

About two strides after Mars you started the curl,
Asteroids bumping you.
(But it was legal; the ball wasn't in the air.)
You used their bumping, letting it ride you into the outcurl
Past Jupiter.
(O you were beautiful!)

And then it was just smooth running
On Uranus, Neptune and deep safety Pluto.

And all this space travelling, this horror of vacuum,
All of it in faith that somehow out in all that terror
There would be a ball to make connections with.

My left arm always speaks at least a weak and wobbly love,
At best a spiralling affection.

Why Jack Butler Is An Occasional Junk Reader,
or,
The Jaws Of A Dilemma

Because junk trembles
In a rough direction
Toward heaven, our home.

Where the girl
Reunites
Part by part
And she runs
In the moon
And makes love
On the beach
And the shark's
Jaws are fed
By the parts
Of the girl
Who makes love
All the while
In the moon
On the beach

The Whole Damned Universe: For Larry Johnson

Call it gorged eel.
Call it Sammy's Slambo, or,
If you so desire,
Call it Jay Bob's Cream and Eat.

There's nothing in the world
Explains the world
And nothing gets you or me
A titsworth nearer truth.

Explore the texts of yore,
Remember that Seurat, Chirico
Get closer to the thing almost
Than long-armed women
Or muezzins in the minarets,
That Mallarmé ate cream of wheat
For many long, apache, slender moons.

When your studies end,
I am your friend.

For Sally

At first it is a portrait,
Careful in its lines —
The artist has kept the photographic faith.
He has planned a modern strategy:
It is dark and it is turning darker there,
A promise of a modern, cosmic music
And a time of no clouding, brightening atmosphere.

You are the feminine dream in all this,
Or, rather, a strange emanation of you,
A hint of benevolence in the eyes,
But the rest is cold mythic.
The face tapers thinward.
The hair spins oppositely from the crown's middle.
The ears are jet perfect.
The red pants say only the littlest bit about fire
(For this is cold, mythic fire).

Of course you're telling us, the viewers, something
Beyond the spoken or the chance for speaking.
Something I can't say,
You can't say,
Something sayable only in the picture:
The dead, everlasting you.

Wayne's Cream Wheat Poem

"Cream wheat, cream wheat," quoth Wayne.
So a panda bear took him into the courtyard
Of Casa de Alicia in far Tampico where the stars turned.

In the hot, doomed land,
Doomed, he thought of Kansas and wheat and creamed
      wheat.
It cooled his lips.

They creamed a man in Chapultepec, Señor.
He read it in the paper.
Wheat soothed him.

Wayne was intelligent.
He ate hot tamales in Mexico City,
And understood wheat and Iowa.

And always it was wheat,
It was running, it was smooth in his heart.
It hurt him softly in his gut.

Finally it broke his heart.
It got his goat.
He babbled.

"Cream wheat, cream wheat."
So a panda bear took him into the courtyard
And whipped the shit out of him.

Written At My Grandmother's Graveside

O, Bella, I see you in the autumn leaves,
In the turning year, I see you turning, Bella.
I see now you have turned again as I sit here
By the flower-drenched new grave.
O, Bella, I hear you in the eerie hall,
I feel your flashlight making sure
We are drunk cardplayers instead of burglars.

The railroad track runs straight beyond here, Bella.
Your life becomes a rounded poem at last.
O, Bella, at the last they say you wereene.

They say you turned down all those shabby suitors —
The needles, the oxygen, those shiny trickeries
That offered you a poor and bitter marriage:
More old, enfeebled life.

O, Bella, the streetlamps at last became
The sun and moon in your age-dark eyes.

I will carry you away from here, Bella.
I will bear you away from here, Bella.
I will not let this ground have all of you

Quite yet.

I am leaving now, Bella.
O, Bella, I am bearing you somewhere in my bones.

While Watching A Fixed Cat Trying

Our old, fixed male cat
Is trying to please
Our younger cat,
An unfixed female.

Acting vestiginously,
Out of memory
And perhaps something
That comes near love,
He is grinding uselessly,

Unless there be a grace
That lets a cat in heat
Know a good try
When she feels one.

Kimpeliana,
or,
A Program For The Emulation
Of A Renaissance Man

I am in a lighted room, trying to become Ben Kimpel.
Ninety years for the novels, five for the medieval
Romances. Ten for the slightly shaky Russian.
Oh, I will need a stern, an almost Prussian
Rigor for Icelandic and Mandarin Chinese.
To date I can report only that my handwritten g's
And y's grow daily more and more like his.
A thousand years and I will take the Kimpel quiz
They give on some far snow-capped, dancing mountain
In the cobwebbed building next the Pierian fountain.

Haunting The Winerunner

Poetry has always started here,
In some misunderstanding
Of someone's will or wish or voice.

The world spoke sanity at them.
They didn't hear or choose to hear.
God became divinest rape.
The air grew alcoholic.

They filled the world with imprecisions of the world.
They warmed death over,
Rearranged the flowers,
Rebuilt joy's engines.

Armed in bright gloves, I stood at dirty dishes.
My son was at toys in our kitchen's corner.
Over the dryer my wife and his mother
Told of the bulldog's taunting the Weimaraner.

PART THREE:
THE PROFESSION OF ENGLISH

An American English Teacher
Foresees His Craft

At six o'clock I squat in the bathroom,
Donning my contacts. Warm suburban caves
Enclose my wife and son. I feel my muscles
Tight (enough) below me and feel my manhood
Hanging in the underwearless room where I arm my eyes.

Again today I will leave this snugness
To report strange and ancient news of words for food.
I feel my fathers in my blood, feel them chasing
What must have baffled them even as they survived
In it and from it — the sabre-toothed tiger.

English Teachers In The Old West

Someday, Gilbert, old partner, it's gonna be
Me and you in chaps and spurs in a dark and dizzy
Bar in far Juarez. We'll belt down red top,
Guzzle sarsaparilla, down beans and sop
With rusty bread the hottest sauce
They got and leave the bar with casual tosses
Of our ponchos as we take the parching fields,
Only to have the drop got on us by words of steel
From a pair of blazing desperadoes, Walter
Line and his trusty sidekick, Slim Halter:
"Drop your poetic impulses and reach for the ground,"
Comes the command, a leaden, deadened sound.

After Having Read Malcolm Cowley's Account Of Hart Crane's Visit To His Bed

He woke to find the poet naked in his bed
Between his wife and him, a hand on each.
He woke. The poet silently arranged
Himself and left the moon-fraught room.

Unprinted wonder of the sleeping couple!
The poet glimpsed a vast and dense material.
He didn't publish what he found,
Which must have lain beyond the artistry of sound.

The Renaissance Humanities Course
Multiple Choice Mid-Term Exam:
Assorted Answers

Pietà was a pope, and, as for Fresco,
Well, Fresco was, like *nouveau riche*, a higher
Class of people. Gesualdo played the lyre
(Or was it lute?) and wrote *The Prince*. Reynaldo
Felt that Palestrina killed the king, though
More and Folly believed the palace fire
Was caused by the Venetian-Munster Choir,
Which sang the "Praise of Folly." Donatello
Wrote "The Birth of Venus," while Erasmus
Taught Raphael to sculpt like Henry Aaron.
Gesso, Duke of Earl (or was it Baron?),
Composed a *branle* on the printing press.
Messina bas-reliefed Savonarola.
Da Vinci made, I think, the first Victrola.

Alphabetical Line Index of Famous
Renaissance Persons, Places and Things

Small Kafkaesque

What if you're one of the ones
Who fall to smallest Kafkaesque,
A tiny rupture barely buckling reality's skin,
Barely moving in normalcy's womb?

Unconfirmed in weirdness,
You teach your English classes,
Moving through the great weird lives
Of men in books.

Only every morning,
Instead of your paper on the lawn,
It's an empty Falstaff beer can
For which you pay your daily rates,
A dime a throw.

You conform.
You bring it in.
You flatten it out with a hammer.
You read it.

If this will keep
The Joseph K
Event away,
Okay.

So you read it, and eat
Your cereal,
Topped with hot bananas.

Jane Austen

Jane's bones now,
Who used to limn a prose
So light, so sweet

I would read it, exclaiming
All the way, I'd say,

"Susan, listen to this."
Susan'd listen to it.

Jane Austen's bones now.
Pachelbel's in his grave, too.

(And who sang better than these two?)

Say to Jane, say, "Jane,
Pick me up, take me where
Your home is." Jane, like Tina, say,

"Sho thing, nigger luv."

Jane say, "In an absence of Napoleon
And French Revolution, in a linen
Of sly wit and fine syntax."

O I was ready for all that absence.

"Are you black enough
To dig my subtle soul,
White boy," Jane say.

After Reading A Wicked French Novel

All day I have read *Liaisons Dangereuses*.
Heart has fled; I am sick at soul.
Reason must die, and should; she has bred
Too many wicked children, too few good.

PART FOUR:
AMATEUR METAPHYSICS

Dialogues With God

God said, "Herman,
I got this religious nut
For you. Teach him
A thing or two." Herman said,
"Lord, this works a hardship
On me, Boss!" God said,
"Bear your cross."

Jack said, "God,
You've blown my mind,
Emptied me." God said,
"Jack, I've got the cure:
Eat three Vienna sausages,
Fill in the aperture."

Unmanned before manhood
By my Baptist sweetheart,
Polly Curry, who boasted
Publicly at sixteen
Of having never been kissed,
I cried to God, who said,
"That's a hot number
You got there, Johnny."
I said, "God, that's not funny."
God said, "yes it is."

We Took Her For A Smoky Madre Maybe . . .

The raped ape screamed in the sunny jungle.
Deep was his gloom, deep was the gloom
Of the jungle in sun, for the sun
Plastered patterns on the ferns
And laid a horrid weave on time.

In time we came to see the horrid weave
The sun and its daddy laid on the jungle floor.
In time we came to see it
As not-our-father, Nada Padre.

The moon's heart ticked a little longer —
Smoky madre — but enough of us
Have seen it as something unpersonifiable

On the floors of kitchens late at night
In the homes of artists, art professors,
All the hangers-on-to-order-under-chaos.

It comes to tell how cold it is and dumb,
This erstwhile angry fragment,
This sad-stepping, inconstant chandelier of yore.

The Kingdom Of God,
Not To Mention Numerous Other Things,
Is Within You,
or *Eternity Verified*

Whatever touches you is in you.
Remember the guy who punched you in the nose?
Your eyes took in the nearing fist.
Your nose registered the blow
On a small, involved seismograph.

I know a man who has been to the South Pole
And read my poems. Incredible orgy:
My poems are in the South Pole,
The South Pole's in my poems.
I'm in the man, the man's in me.
Finally we have verified eternity.

Infinity of in, within —
And how could all this ever end?

Two Sex Poems, One With Religious Significance

1. The Dismal Ditches

   I have been in some dismal ditches,
   Seeking the rhythms of a higher pornography,
   The soul's palpable thrill.

2. Slightly Contra Freud

   I would like to believe
   That crazy animal motion,
   Stirring as it is,
   Is not the heart
   Of all our gestures.

Dining At The Vishnu

"I'll have the god."
"With or without attributes, sir?"
"With. And coffee, please."
"Thank you, sir."

God After Breakfast

This strange and riddling ghost he tells us of,
This old skywalker, this bleak aurora
He tells us of. He comes before us
After danish, coffee, orange juice
And tells us of this thing, this god that matters
More than all the world that he can see:
The wife, the silver poplars, golden days.

It is a bad adultery.

Bad Animals On The Baltic

"St. Vitus converted the heathen of Rugen in the Baltic; but a few generations later, fresh missionaries found a population of relapsed heathens, who honoured their earlier apostle rather in breach than in observance of his teaching. They had erected an idol which they called Swantovit; this they worshipped with human sacrifice, preferably of Christians."

— G. G. Coulton

They weren't the first or last to turn
a living god to stone.
The human reflex is to catch a deity
and never let it go,

to fix it in a stone or word,
to halter it in terms and tones

and bash the heads of those
whose terms and tones are not
the terms and tones of those
who bash the heads of those

whose...

This round has run most redly
ever since the life of God
was caged in crippled, human zoos.

The Baltic's coastline's longer than we want to know.

When Jesus Walked The Waters

How?
You were and are the Son of God and so could
Walk the waters. They were real live waters,
Though, with crests and dips and stinking foam.
You sweetened them. That's easy for me.
You walked them. How? Did you select
A surfer's style and slide and glide,
Arms balanced one against the other?
O did you hold your arms out, O my God?
Or did you perpetrate a ghostly surface
Two feet or so below the cruel crests
And slosh along, a weird pedestrian?

I cannot see it. I would not see it.
The taste is gross that in our filmy age
Would try to film it. It is a vulgar thought,
My Dear, if thought too closely on.

You planted me deep in the sad loam,
The black, rich history of earth, safe
From your fireworks, stunts and freak shows.
I know that in the circus you got somehow
Beyond the circus. I know you brought it off,
Lord God. I can't imagine how.

Jesus Loves You. But Does God Love You?

Jesus loves you. But does God love you?
Of course Jesus loves you,
The undiscriminating creep.

Love burns brightly for a while,
But hate — God love it — sparkles
Endlessly. Jesus loves you.

But does God love you?
God the Purple.
God the Biter.

A raging stream bears all life away.
Jesus loves you.
But does God love you?

Poem From A Godly Angle

God wakes each morning mortified.
There are spots of time, some say
(Immeasurable to man, so small are they),
In which God naps away from pain.
For in these spots no man bleeds,
No animal cries, no plant is plucked
(So small they are).

He has a way to savor them,
To draw out their tiny
Infinitesimality.

Saved, But

I am home now,
Home from the sad, pocked earth,
In one of the many mansions.

I am saved, but
I have a longing,
A wish for the fullthroated loving
I never did quite do
On the earth, the right place.

Here I am bliss forever,
Saved, but I have
A longing.

It has made a tiny tear, a small run
In the shimmering fabric of heaven.

God Goes Through The Hurt

All the grainy, pebbled pain,
The seamy, rutted, jutted, jagged
Rusty trombone noise of loss, the ragged
Hurt that tunnels in your deepest veins:

What if God goes through it, too,
Whose locus is within the world, behind
The scenes, who seems at times almost beyond
That bitch whose torn complainings wounded you?

Not that God quite holds your bleeding hand,
But, rather, recognizes trembling spots of time
As integers of his own building, rhymes
That crash in you, but in his kingdom band.

PART FIVE:
AUTOBIOGRAPHY

Seven Ways To Prune A Grapefruit

Harry Johnson's got his highschool sweater on, bop bop.
Mad Jack Ainsworth's got my ice cream cone.
Roy Payne can't find anybody his size to pick on:
These are the seven ways to prune a grapefruit.

A Crab In The Creamworks

Something loathsome is happening
To a single cheerio
In the fogged dishwater.

A crab is loose in the lovely,
Dished, *au gratin* creamworks.

I dreamt a throbbing,
An exquisite mechanics
Of creamworks, as if,
From Orange, Texas to far Cathay
There could perhaps be a system,
A vegetable algebra
Of creamworks, a calculus,
Heart-motored, so that all
The area under the wavy line
Could be graphed, determined
In uncrabbed, creamworked terms.

What If

I were walking
To school some starry morning
And a man shot my head to pieces
With a gun?

Would my brain
In that hallowed, preshattered second
Tell me,
It's all right.
You got your head blown off
With as much (and unmuch)
Dignity
As just about anybody?

Torn Counsel °

Wistaria looping my lonely heart,
Marigolds burning my brain,
I saw a grave by the water's bright edge,
Heard a glad voice calling my name:
"Go deep. Go to the bone.
Polish your life with the marble-veined world,
Blister your heart on a whetstone
Of rage, charm rage to love
(O deep, deep to the bone you must go),
Tone it to calm."

The kind sun was wasting my life.
A worm was consuming my colorful brain.
A withering voice spoke a blazing command:
"Deep. Go deep to the bone."

The Day He Found Out
He And All The Thugs
Are Distant Kin

That guy that runs the filling
Station's not worth killing.
He's a frog-faced pig, a blank-browed,
Spilling-gutted slob, and not like us, like us . . . .

This rage runs small in the world's rhythms,
A tiny, minor spasm.
Still, it is Dachau, Siberia and Wounded Knee
In microcosm.

People Used To Say

People used to say, when they saw
Me coming, "Look, here comes
The nicest guy in the world."

They don't say that anymore.
Lately I've been reading several
Small books on the fur trade

And related topics with voracious
Intensity. They don't say that anymore.
That's one thing's for damn sure.

My God, the blood the beaver
Bled, the flood of small print
La Salle and Coronado wrought.

Seven cities of gold
And all that golden beaver blood.
They don't say that anymore.

Second Semester Freshman

Cornwallis, of course, and brandied fruit
And a smattering of foreign tongues.
The songbirds in some Yeatsy tree
Singing of rainless lands, the crabs
Of time, choked on their villainy,
And, later, something softer than a womb.

A pleasant crowding followed by a thin
Remorse — the line I didn't get quite right,
The razor that I never did quite grip.
A thin remorse, a balmy panic,
A tinily attempted pushing away
Of this web that seems to hang
Before my very eyes, this vast
And vulgar temple of unknowing,
This gauze of imprecision,
This ineluctable and constant
Being what I am:
A second semester freshman.

Nightwood

Well, let's see —
His father hits the tree —
No —
I hit the tree at the same time he pretends to hit it —
Is that right?
Well, let's try it.

Love

Best love boils to imagination.
We would shriek "Love!"
But our best chance to say it
Lies in woodsmoke and wild hope.

That stranger
Rounding the corner
In his cream blue sports car
With the Great Dane in the small back seat:
The best I can hope for him, love for him
Is some windy, mindy adventure —
That something of him will zoom out of here
To Pocatello, Idaho or, better, Tremonton, Utah.

The Poet

John Wink received his B.A. from the University of Southern Mississippi and his M.A. and Ph.D. from the University of Arkansas. He is a member of Phi Beta Kappa. Currently John is Associate Professor of English at Ouachita Baptist University in Arkadelphia, Arkansas, where he recently was voted "Outstanding Teacher of the Year" by the student body.

John lives with his wife, Susan, and son, Gene.